Jenny Mosley's
Top Tips for

Midday

Supervisors

Positive Press

Published in 2011 by:
Positive Press Ltd
28A Gloucester Road
Trowbridge
Wiltshire BA14 0AA

Telephone: 01225 719204
Fax: 01225 712187
E-mail: positivepress@jennymosley.co.uk
Website: www.circle-time.co.uk

Text © Jenny Mosley
Reprinted 2014, 2015
ISBN 978-1-904-866-46-6

Printed in the U.K. by www.heronpress.co.uk

Contents

Introduction

Being a lunchtime supervisor isn't always easy, but it can be a very valuable and rewarding job. Lunchtimes and playtimes allow the children the opportunity to relax away from the pressures of the classroom, build positive relationships and have fun. For some children though they can also bring stress and additional pressures.

Within your role, supervision is only one aspect of the many jobs that you do from being a play leader to agony aunt! However, although the work may be demanding at times, it can also give you great pleasure to build positive relationships with the children and watch the shyer ones blossom and grow in confidence. You can, with a good team:

• Help to produce an outside environment that both children and adults enjoy being in

• Help to create happy and calm playtimes

• Help children to resolve differences and play cooperatively

• Help to boost the confidence of withdrawn children

• Help to make the playground a safe place for all children

• Help to produce a positive atmosphere in the dining area

• Encourage children to use their imaginations in play

• Teach children new games and activities for their enjoyment

Getting to know the children

The most important aspect of your role is getting to know the children that you will be supervising. Some schools match up supervisors to a specific class so that the children and teacher can develop close and trusting relationships with you.

Take time to chat and show that you are friendly and approachable, that you are there to look after them and that you care about each individual. The children in your care will come from many different backgrounds, with very differing experiences of family life. Some you will find easy to like and get on with, whilst with others it will be more difficult, but it is your role to reach out to every child in your care. You have to remember at all times, that your attitude and behaviour will have an impact on the children and determine how they respond to you.

It will help you to know what children look for and like in their lunchtime supervisors. The following list was compiled from interviews with children all over the country -they were very decisive about what they did and didn't want.

According to the children, the best lunchtime supervisors were:

Smiley and happy

Fair and didn't have favourites

Friendly and warm

Respectful and polite

Calm and didn't shout

Fun and had a laugh

Interested in what they did

Sympathetic and kind

The children also said that the best supervisors:

> *Made them feel safe*
>
> *Didn't make personal or sarcastic remarks*
>
> *Gave praise and rewards*
>
> *Didn't pre-judge situations*
>
> *Listened to both sides in a dispute*
>
> *Helped sort out differences*
>
> *Noticed anyone who was sad or lonely*

And above all: They made the children feel cared for and liked!

Be smiley

A friendly face is always more welcoming and inviting. A stern expression can lead children to believe that you are cross with them or may not want to be bothered by them. It can make them think that you are unapproachable.

Have fun

Being fun is like having a personal magnet that will attract the children to you. Fun is also very infectious and easily spread to others. If you are willing to joke, laugh, play and have fun, the children will flock to you.

Play games

If you know any traditional playground games or are willing to learn some that you can teach and play with the children, they will be happily and enjoyably occupied and seek out your company.

Take time to chat

Being willing to chat is a very important quality. Children love to tell their news, talk about what they have done and anything exciting about their families. You can learn about their hobbies and interests, the pets they have and the outings they go on and show your interest in them by commenting to the children about something they have told you previously. Showing that you have remembered their news will demonstrate to the children that you care about them.

Avoid prying

Whilst children love to talk about themselves and their lives, it is important to steer clear of prying about personal domestic issues and never breach confidentiality and gossip with other adults about any personal items told by the children. It will be rare, but if a child does tell you something that you feel uneasy about, there are designated members of staff who deal with child protection issues and who you should tell your concerns to.

Be sensitive

Take care not to make personal remarks that might embarrass children in front of their friends. They can be very sensitive about their appearance, especially if they are aware that they don't quite fit in. A comment that you might see as harmless teasing could be adding to the negative feelings they have about themselves.

Be consistent

Everybody has their 'off' days, but try and be consistent with the children in your care. If you have mood swings and are happy and approachable one day, but grumpy and stand-offish the next, the children will become confused and unsure of you. They might then be wary of coming to you for a chat or even help.

Show that you are available

Make sure that the children know you are available and approachable. If you are on duty with another adult, it's very tempting to stand together and become involved in chatting. Try and walk round the playground and call out small comments and greetings to the children as you pass them. This will show that you are ready and willing to talk to them.

Keep an eye open

As you move around the playground, keep an eye open on all areas, especially if some are rather hidden away. Make a mental note of what the children are doing, look for any potential problems or children who are on their own and looking lonely.

Nip problems in the bud

If you see any situations that look problematic, try and nip them in the bud. Sometimes distraction can be the best way to dispel trouble, so it is worth approaching with greetings and general chat initially, rather than going in with guns blazing. If the situation hasn't really developed into a quarrel, a conversation about the weather, an event in school etc can take the children's minds off their problem and defuse the situation.

Avoid having obvious favourites

It can be difficult not to have favourites as there will always be children you are more drawn to than others. However, in your role as a lunchtime supervisor, you are working and should not allow personal likes and dislikes to influence how you treat the children. They all need to feel liked and valued. If you feel that you are having a real problem in liking a particular child, make a focus of getting to know them better and find a positive aspect to their character. It can help to turn things round.

Know the rules

Make sure that you know all the school rules that apply to the children in your care. If you are uncertain about them it can make you inconsistent in deciding what is right and wrong, undermine your authority or make it difficult to resolve a dispute. Ask the senior management if they can be put up on the walls outside.

Be open-minded

Keep an open mind when you are dealing with any incident or dispute. Take the time to find out what really happened by listening to both sides of the story and even questioning onlookers, rather than jumping to conclusions. Making a hasty decision could be the wrong one and lead to an injustice.

Remember praise and rewards motivate

Try and balance any 'tellings off' with praise and rewards. You don't want to be seen as someone who only gets cross. Find opportunities to commend good behaviour and give out stickers and other rewards, especially to children who find it difficult to behave well. Praise and reward is far more effective than criticism and punishment. Also, remember to show children what they should be doing by being polite and modelling good behaviour.

Be fair

Treat all children equally and fairly. Check out the school's sanction system and always give the same consequence for the same offence. Don't treat some children more harshly because they are 'always causing trouble' or let others off because they are 'usually good'. How you treat the children will affect how they feel towards you.

Stay calm

If you have to tell children off, stay calm and avoid shouting. Some children, who are unused to loud, angry voices can become really frightened when someone shouts and the bad memory can stay with them for a long time, even when they are not the person being shouted at. If you stay calm and don't lose your temper, you will be able to think and act more clearly.

Know the management systems

Make sure that you know the correct procedures and consequences to use when you need to respond to bad behaviour and be aware of whom you should go to if you need help. It is much better to bring in another member of staff than struggle to stay in control and lose authority.

> *The most important thing is to be a safe and trustworthy ally for the children in your care!*

Helping children to behave well

Children need to understand that rules are made to offer guidance and show them how to behave, so that everyone can feel happy and safe in their environment. Children come from many different backgrounds with all sorts of boundaries and rules. Some will live in homes with strict carers and rigid behaviour boundaries whilst others live with carers who are more relaxed about what the children can and can't do. Others still live in chaotic households where boundaries change all the time and what is acceptable one day will be punished the next. For some children, keeping to the rules in school is not a problem. The rules may be similar to the ones they have at home or they may be more willing to do as they are told. Other children may seem to find it impossible to keep the rules and behave in a manner that is acceptable and safe. The adults in the school need to be sure and consistent about the rules systems that operate in order to create a whole school, united approach.

.

Golden Rules

Golden rules inform the moral values of a school and are discussed and drawn up in Circle Time. Below are the Golden Rules that I advocate for the playground and these should be prominently displayed throughout the school.

Playground Golden Rules

We are gentle	*We don't hurt others*
We are kind and helpful	*We don't hurt anybody's feelings*
We play well with others	*We don't spoil others' games*
We care for the playground	*We don't damage or spoil anything*
We listen	*We don't interrupt*
We are honest	*We don't cover up the truth*

We keep the playground safety rules

Happy playtime rules

It is a good idea to have a set of specific rules also that focus on routines. An example is shown below.

Playtime Rules

When the bell rings we stand still
We play together and look after each other
We let other children get on with their games
We give equipment to Playground Friends
at the end of playtime
We tell an adult if we feel sad or lonely

Safety rules

These rules, agreed by the staff, should be displayed on a large sign and be clearly visible to all children. An example is given below.

> ## Safety Rules
>
> **Keep within the football boundaries**
> **Only use softballs in this area**
> **Stay on the ground – do not climb the railings**
> **Do get permission to go inside**

Remind children of the rules when they are behaving inappropriately and check that they actually understand what a particular rule means. Then ask them to explain to you how they have broken that rule.

Choosing your words carefully will show that whilst you disapprove of certain behaviours, you don't disapprove of the child.
For example, rather than say, "You are very naughty to throw that toy" you could say, "Throwing that toy was dangerous as it could have hurt someone." And instead of saying, "You are a bad tempered boy." you could say, "Losing your temper made you punch Lola, which broke our Golden Rule of being gentle"

Zoning the playground

Zoning the playground is a simple strategy for helping children to behave well. Creating different areas for different activities provides additional interest and helps avoid conflicts of interests, such as when one group of children want to use an area for one activity and another group wishes to use the same space for a different activity.

Zoning will enable you to make better use of the available space and ensure that the playground is shared more fairly, so that certain games such as football don't dominate the playing area.

Boundaries between different areas can be created using paint, shrubs, cones or chalk. The different zones can be used for a variety of activities, examples of which are described below.

Craze of the week

A different craze can be taught to the children each week e.g. hula hoops, marbles, cats cradle, soft ball game, playground cricket. Crazes may mean that new equipment has to be purchased and perhaps your school's PTA could contribute to this. Crazes are wonderful because they teach children new skills and encourage them to share and co-operate with one another. Playground friends can demonstrate the new craze each week in an assembly and then help the children learn any techniques, with your assistance, in the playground.

After a week the equipment is packed away until the next time it is required and a new craze is introduced.

Traditional games zone

Schools are starting to re-introduce traditional playground games e.g. stuck in the mud. You could join forces with playground friends to teach these to the children. In some schools, a couple of lunchtime supervisors hold regular games sessions that focus on one class at a time, teaching and playing games with the children that they can then take into the playground.

Quiet zone

A quiet zone, often somewhere sheltered such as a garden, can be equipped with benches and seats or carpet tiles, and used by the children for reading, playing board games, filling in colouring or activity books or just sitting and chatting quietly.

Make-believe zone

A dressing up box with a variety of costumes will encourage imaginative play. Often a letter home with a plea for suitable garments will provide sufficient items to fill a box.

Music and dance zone

Children can be very enthusiastic about a music and dance zone and will offer plenty of suggestions about the music that they like. The relevant equipment can be stored in a large plastic box and kept in the store cupboard. Children may like to organise a talent contest to show-case their singing and dancing.

Painted games zone

Games involving a painted number line or alphabet are both educational and fun. You could also paint a draughts board and use with giant pieces or a hop-scotch grid.

Construction zone

An area can be cordoned off for use with construction toys and other small equipment. Children can create tracks for cars or build models.

Football zone

It is important that routines and regulations are established so that football doesn't take over the playing area. Also, there can be a tendency for the game to be dominated by older, stronger players which may present problems. Some schools have two football zones, one for younger and the other for older players. Other schools get round this problem by scheduling different ages or sexes to use the football pitch on different days of the week.

There may need to be specific rules about who chooses teams to avoid disputes and clear guidelines about what constitutes fair play. Involving the children in this process is a good idea as they are more likely to adhere to rules if they have had a hand in making them.

Friendship stop zone

This is an area in the playground where lonely children can wait for a Playground Friend to come and talk to them and help them find someone to play with. Some schools provide a brightly painted bench that says 'Friendship Stop'. Providing an area such as this shows that the school has a caring ethos and values friendship and inclusion.

Encouraging good behaviour

Try to remember that praise and positive comment really work better than punishment. Think how you feel when someone says something nice to or about you. You are more likely to have positive feelings about that person and want to please them. Stating a belief in a child can also have a good effect, especially with younger children e.g. "I know that you are a good girl and can behave really well." Giving incentives also helps, firstly because children love to receive them and secondly, because being able to distribute rewards adds status and authority to your position in the school.

Some valuable incentives that encourage children to behave well are outlined below.

Stickers
Readily available and easy to use, stickers give instant positive feedback to children. They can be awarded for:

> *having good table manners*
> *lining up sensibly*
> *playing well with others*
> *trying to improve*

Lunchtime certificates
In some schools, certificates to commend children for behaving well during lunchtimes are awarded in an assembly, to give them added prestige. In other schools, the lunchtime supervisors prefer to award the certificates themselves, handing them out in the dining hall at the end of the week, once the children have finished eating

Lunchtime helper badges
Responsibility is a proven incentive to promote good behaviour as it helps children to feel valued and important. Badges denote the children's status for a variety of tasks such as:

> *Wiping tables*
> *Helping to clear litter in the playground*
> *Fetching and putting away playground equipment*
> *Helping to organise games and activities*
> *Monitoring classrooms and corridors*
> *Teaching games to younger children*
> *Organising a quiet area*

Special table of the week

Prepare a special table that is dressed with a cloth and a vase of dried/artificial flowers. Children who have been helpful or behaved well at lunchtimes are chosen to sit at this table and each may be given a spare invitation so that they enjoy the privilege of inviting a guest to join them

Golden Stars of the Week

A special board is decorated and prepared with this heading. Each week the names or photographs of children who have behaved particularly well at lunchtimes are displayed.

Book of Praise

A large, attractively bound book makes a super Book of Praise in which you can write the names of those children who have behaved well during lunchtimes. The names can be subsequently read out in an assembly.

Raffle

Children are given a raffle ticket for behaving well and at the end of the week, all the tickets are collected and a raffle is held. The child with the winning ticket is awarded a prize or a privilege.

Lining up tickets

To encourage children to line up calmly and sensibly at the end of playtimes, tickets or tokens can be awarded to classes that achieve this with a suitable reward such as a game or additional Golden Time.

Class Link

If you are linked to a particular class, it is a good idea to spend some time each week having an informal chat with the children to share good news or discuss any issues. This will help to develop good relationships between you and the children.

Responding to poor behaviour

Children need to understand that good behaviour is necessary for everyone's safety and happiness and that there are consequences when they do not behave well. However, there will always be some incidents related to poor behaviour that you will have to deal with. The sanctions that you use should be clear, consistently applied and shared by all the lunchtime supervisors. If you are not sure of the sanctions that operate within your school, you should check with other members of staff.

Help cards
The use of Help cards is a valuable system to provide assistance and ensure everyone's safety. All lunchtime supervisors are issued with laminated Help cards. If an incident arises that they feel unable to cope with, they can give the card to a trustworthy child to take to an agreed place such as the office or staff room, in order to call for additional assistance.

Loss of Golden Time
Golden Time is essentially a celebration of the children's ability to keep the Golden Rules. If this system happens in your school, a loss of this privilege is an ideal consequence for breaking rules. Golden Time is a set period each week during which all the children who have behaved well can enjoy a range of special and enjoyable activities. Breaking the rules results in a loss of part of this time. If, after you have given a child a verbal warning, they continue to break a rule, their name is noted and given to their class teacher. The teacher deducts 5 or 10 minutes off their Golden Time, during which they must sit with a timer and consider both the rule that they have broken and how they can avoid doing this again in the future. Using this system as a sanction, promotes a whole school response and teaches the children that the same values operate in all parts of the school.

Incident form
When an incident involves verbal or physical abuse, the details should be recorded in a special book or on an incident form. You may be asked to complete this and you may need a witness in order to corroborate your account. The form is then handed in at the office or given to the Head Teacher.
The Head Teacher will follow up the incident by arranging a meeting with the pupil to discuss what happened and obtain their signature against the details. Parents are subsequently notified and sanctions put in place.

Children beyond

Some children find it hard to keep the rules and behave well. These children persistently break the rules and are beyond the usual range of incentives and sanctions that work with the majority. Some may have conditions that make it difficult for them to fit in, whilst others have emotional or behavioural problems. Children such as these often get into fights and arguments as they cannot cope with the lack of structured time during lunchtimes and on windy days they can really 'loop the loop'. A few children are unable to cope with lunchtimes because they have a disorder on the autistic spectrum such as Asperger's Syndrome. This can make it very difficult for them to cope with time away from the routines of the classroom. They may also not be able to mix well and get on with other children. If you think that a particular child is having real trouble fitting in at lunchtimes, talk to their teacher. Where children have problems mixing with others, it will not help to label them as naughty. They continue to repeat poor behaviour because they are unable to change without additional help and need support to enable them to feel better about themselves and to get on with others.

Self-help story books

These can provide a very helpful intervention as they focus a child's attention on their behaviour and encourage them to reflect on how it affects others. It is important to observe the child and note down specific behaviours rather than general statements e.g. 'You kicked Milo' rather than 'You behaved badly'. Children are given strategies to help them cope or a safe place that they can go to and calm down. Children keep their story books with them and look at them regularly to remind themselves of how they should behave. An example is shown below.

Lola's Story

My name is Lola and I am good and kind.

If someone accidentally knocks me, says something hurtful or looks at me in a way that I don't like, I sometimes get angry.

When I am angry I feel hot and bothered and clench my fists.

When I get angry I might want to hit or kick or swear at someone.

Hitting and kicking is not kind and I should not do it.

Hitting and kicking hurts people and makes them upset and sometimes angry with me.

Swearing at people is not kind and I should not do it.

Swearing makes people upset and hurts their feelings. It makes them sad and sometimes they get angry with me.

When I am angry or upset I should try to remember to do the right thing.

I could:

Move away from the situation that is making me upset or angry.
                    Or
Tell an adult
                    Or
Take a deep breath and count to 10
                    Or
Go to my safe place, sit quietly and read a book or draw a picture or do some colouring

I can keep my story book with me at school and look at it.

Reading my story book will remind me of the right thing to do when I feel angry or upset.

My name is Lola and I am good and kind.

Target cards

Target cards are another useful idea to encourage good behaviour. The child's targets are written on a card and signed each day that they are achieved. Targets need to be specific e.g. 'I will go and tell a supervisor if I feel angry with someone.' 'I will not hit another person.'

The targets should be reviewed regularly and a 'Well Done' certificate signed by you and the child's teacher sent home to inform the parents of the child's success. Targets may need to be revisited at some time in the future if the behaviour recurs.

Specific interventions

Sometimes a child need intervention on their behalf if they are unable to cope with a specific situation. For example a child with a disorder on the autistic spectrum may find the noise and bustle of lining up for lunch very difficult. In this instance, the problem could be solved by allowing the child to leave the classroom a minute or two earlier than the other children and being at the front of the queue. It is important to consider whether the child's environment is having an impact on their behaviour.

The community task-force

A community task-force can be used when a child really can't cope with playtimes. This involves a small group of children (3-7) who help with a variety of projects. The group can include other children who are able to model good behaviour. The group may be set up by the Head Teacher, SENCo or a teacher and members of staff are required to be responsible for a 30 minute session on a rota basis. You may be asked to help supervise the group or assist with the tasks. Jobs undertaken could include restoring furniture, maintenance work around the school or making items to sell, perhaps for the school summer fete or Christmas bazaar. You may have an interest or hobby that the children would enjoy being involved with.

During the sessions, it is important that 'children beyond' are given positive attention from the adults that will help build their self-esteem and make them feel worthy and valued.

Lunchtime club

Some schools provide a lunchtime club that is organised and run by two lunchtime supervisors. The club provides activities and games and a safe haven for children who find lunchtimes difficult. Places at the club are alloted to specific children by the teachers, but there should also be some spare places as well. The other children can then all have a turn at joining in the club if they so choose.

Individual playtime programme

This is a structured programme that lasts 6-12 weeks and covers all playtimes, providing additional support for a 'child beyond'.

Children work or play with an adult in a small group (3-4). Both you and the child can choose another child to join the group on a day to day basis. The programme should include a selection of activities and special responsibilites such as :

> ***board games - jig-saws - colouring***
> ***puzzles - playground games***
> ***lunchtime duties such as wiping tables,***
> ***collecting rubbish - taking part in a club***

It is a good idea to gradually re-introduce a child into playtimes, perhaps starting with the last 5 minutes and gradually increasing the time as the child shows that they are able to cope and behave well.

Playtime mentoring

Some schools use playground mentors to help a 'child beyond' behave well. The role of the mentor could be to:

* Be a friend and play with the 'child beyond'

* Help them meet their playground targets

* Help them in their Individual Playtime Programme

* Be part of the task force with them.

Responding to challenging behaviour

Bullying

Bullying, if ignored, can cause suffering to the victims that might result in lifelong emotional problems. Every school is required to have a policy that tackles bullying which will inform you how you should deal with any incidents.
Make sure that you are familiar with the correct responses and procedures, so that a consistent approach is adopted by the whole school.

Be aware of the difference between bullying and squabbles or one-off incidents. Bullying involves deliberate, hurtful behaviour that is repeated over time. It may be physical e.g. hitting, pushing, verbal e.g. name-calling, making malicious comments or indirect e.g. spreading rumours, excluding children from games. The playground can be the place where bullying occurs most due to the freedom it offers and lack of close scrutiny. It is therefore important to be watchful and to respond to any incident immediately. You can then work with members of the teaching staff to help support the victims and the bullies as they may both need to learn different behaviours. Also, peer groups can be enlisted to help sort out problems.

> ***Action against bullying is effective when:***
> ***Time and effort is put into developing the school's***
> ***anti-bullying policy***
> ***and***
> ***The whole school shares the same values and responds***
> ***in the same way to bullying***

An important factor in any anti-bullying campaign is to encourage children to report incidents of bullying against themselves or others. They need to realise that reporting bullying is not telling-tales and is perfectly acceptable, in fact desirable. They also need to know that they can approach staff in confidentiality. These two messages should be relayed to the children frequently.
It is equally important that follow-up action is taken when an incident is reported to reinforce the message that bullying is not tolerated in the school.

Children are often able to supply important details that help to build up an overall picture such as areas where bullying frequently occurs e.g. in the toilets, on the football pitch or times when it is most likely to happen e.g. at the end of the day.

Some helpful ideas to combat bullying are:

- Make sure you patrol the areas frequently where bullying is most likely to occur

- Provide children who bully with plenty of supervised activities to keep them occupied

- Provide victims with a safe place to go

- Take time to obtain the facts and interview both the victim and the child accused of bullying for their accounts of what happened

- Ask witnesses to confirm the details of the event

- Stay calm and don't be drawn into a heated discussion. If you feel that you are becoming annoyed, walk away and count to 10

- Prepare a script of specific questions to ask that will provide the answers that you require. This is called a structured conversation and can be very helpful in providing the information you need

- Introduce changes to reduce opportunities for bullying. For example create playground crazes of the week to provide novel interests, utilize zoning more effectively, introduce new rules about visiting toilets or for the end of the day

Bullying often occurs when children are bored and unoccupied or lack social or friendship skills. Providing plenty of interesting activities, moving around the playground and keeping in touch with the children will help to promote a happy, friendly environment and minimise the occurrence of incidents.

Anger management

When a child loses their temper, it will only escalate the situation if you respond with anger. Losing control of their temper can be as upsetting for the child concerned as for the target of their anger.

Once a child has had an angry outburst, encourage them to walk away from the situation and cool off. Don't attempt to talk things through while a child is in an emotionally charged state, wait until they have calmed down.

Talk through the incident calmly, asking the child to describe what happened and, if they can, describe what triggered the outburst. Explain that everyone becomes angry at times, but they can learn how to deal with their feelings in a way that does not lead to angry outbursts and the consequences that these might bring.

Children need to learn that everyone is responsible for their own behaviour, but they can learn to respond to feelings in a different way.

If other children are deliberately winding a child up in order to make them lose their temper, a class circle time might be required to deal with this, so talk to their teacher.

Teach children the following strategies to help them calm down:

1. Breathe in slowly to the count of 5, hold breath for the count of 5 then breathe out through their nose to the count of 5 and hold again for the count of 5.

2. Breathe slowly and regularly in and out and contract all their muscles so that they are rigid. Breathe out slowly and, at the same time, start to relax their muscles from the feet upwards.

Also, encourage children to seek out and talk to an adult if they feel they are becoming angry or go to a designated quiet area to cool off.

Playground friends

Playground friends are an ideal way of using children's willing helpfulness to your advantage. In order for this scheme to be really effective, it has to be a whole school initiative that is properly organised and monitored. For this reason, a member of staff will need to be in charge of running the scheme.

Regular meetings should be scheduled with the children to discuss how things are going and to resolve any issues that develop. The scheme will involve a variety of jobs that need to be advertised. Children apply for a position and are interviewed by the staff organiser, who will subsequently brief all the successful candidates on what is required of them. They will also need to be reminded that the role requires a commitment for a specified length of time. It is a good idea if each 'friend' takes a turn at all of the jobs on the list. At the end of the specified time, the jobs are re-advertised for new recruits to apply.

The jobs on the list could include:

- Setting tables for lunch
- Clearing tables
- Helping younger children with their lunches
- Organising games in the playground
- Getting out and putting away equipment
- Talking to or playing with lonely children
- Collecting litter from the playground

Letters are sent to parents informing them of the playground friend scheme and the benefits that it brings to the children involved as they are given responsibilities and learn to consider others' well-being.

Benefits of being a playground friend:
It develops a sense of responsibility for their environment and for others
It helps children develop maturity
It helps to build self-esteem and confidence
It helps to foster a caring attitude
It helps children find solutions to playground issues

It helps children understand the reasons for rules within a community
It helps children to learn moral values such as turn taking and sharing.

It is a good idea to introduce a checking system that takes note of a playground friend's absence with an alternative way of fulfilling their role.

Rainy days

There will inevitably be rainy days and wet playtimes when the children are kept indoors. These can be hard work and very trying of your patience if the children are not happily involved. You may even be required to keep an eye on more than one class and this will be a potential time for incidents such as fights to develop. To minimise the risk of any problems during wet playtimes the following issues should be considered:

- Make sure the children have sufficient space in which to play
- Make sure that there are sufficient activities to keep everyone occupied
- Make sure there are sufficient staff to monitor what is happening
- Make sure that noise levels do not become too loud and upset some children.

The best solution is to be well prepared with an interesting and varied selection of toys, games and activities that are kept in a labelled box. In order to maintain some novelty value, wet weather equipment could be passed from class to class each half term on a rota system.

Some ideas of equipment for wet playtimes are:
Comics and magazines, paper, coloured pencils, colouring books, puzzle and word-search books, activity books, board games, story books.

Activity days
From time to time, you could organise a special activity day when it is raining. For example, the children could make their own games such as ludo, snakes and ladders, dominoes and drafts which could be laminated and added to the wet weather equipment box.
They could play a group memory game e.g. I went to the shop and bought…. or I went to the zoo and saw…….
They could play 'Hide the thimble' (or other small object)
They could make a paper picture chain
They could make Easter bonnets
They could play 'Guess my object'. From a selection of displayed objects, one child chooses and thinks of one. The other children ask questions until they have guessed the object. It is then removed from the display.
(For other creative ideas for wet playtimes see resources section)

The dining hall

Most children in the school will eat their lunch in the dining hall, so there needs to be a system that is efficient but unhurried. Rules that apply in this area could be:

> **Rules for lunchtimes**
> **We line up quietly**
> **We walk in the dining hall**
> **We finish what we are eating before we speak**
>
> **We remember to say 'Please' and 'Thank you'**
> **We clear away our rubbish**
> **We put up our hands to ask to leave the dining hall**
> **We talk quietly to the people next to us.**

The rules should be prominently displayed next to the school or Golden Rules in the dining hall. Lining up can create all sorts of issues and needs to be supervised by an adult. If problems arise at this time, they should be discussed by the staff to find a solution. For example, how the classes are called to the line could be changed in order that the line and therefore the wait is never too long. If children have lunchtime clubs to attend, they could be allowed at the front of the queue.

Asking for quiet

A very effective way to gain quiet in the dining hall is to train the children to raise their hands and stop talking when you raise yours. Younger children can also be instructed to place a finger on their lips to help them remember to be silent. A good idea is to use this rule to praise a quiet group of children so that the others take note that being quiet is a positive school value and not a restriction.

Good manners

It is no longer standard practice for families to always eat together around a table and some children may need to be taught how this is done. Class teachers may hold a class circle time with the children to talk about what constitutes good manners and what behaviour might be considered bad mannered. Children can pretend that they are in a fancy restaurant and practice their table manners. Encourage best behaviour by handing out praise and rewards

Slow eaters

A few children may seem to take for ever to eat their lunches and become upset if they are hurried. It may be a good idea to designate one table for slow eaters so that you can begin to clear up the dining hall around them. Some schools give stickers to children who eat well to encourage concentration on the task.

Safety

Accidents can happen, even in the best organised dining halls and playgrounds. Your school should operate agreed procedures in the event that this happens. If you are unsure of what to do in an emergency, ask about the systems in operation. Taking a first aid course may be an option and this will help raise your confidence in responding to accidents. The list of first-aid trained staff should be regularly reviewed to make sure that qualifications are up to date.

Class circle times

You may be able to join a class circle time on occasion, especially if it involves discussion about matters relating to lunchtimes or playtimes. If you are invited, don't be nervous about joining in as this will give you a good opportunity to chat with the children and they will appreciate you being there.

Regular meetings

The calmest and happiest schools have regular meetings between senior management, teachers and midday supervisors. Have a word with them and say you'd be really keen!

Resources

Mosley, J. and Sonnet, H. (2004) Playground Games. Co-operative learning for lively children. Trowbridge: Positive Press

Mosley, J. and Sonnet, H. (2004) Skipping Games. Energetic workouts for lively children. Trowbridge: Positive Press

Mosley, J. and Sonnet, H. (2005) Wet Playtime Games. Rainy day resources for calmer classrooms. Trowbridge: Positive Press

Mosley, J (2011) Craze of the Week Cards. Series 1. Trowbridge: Positive Press

Mosley, J (2012) Craze of the Week Cards. Series 2. Trowbridge: Positive Press

Mosley, J (2012) Ball Games. Series 1 and 2. Trowbridge: Positive Press

Mosley, J (2009) Midday Supervisor Reward Pads. Trowbridge: Positive Press

Mosley, J (2009) Midday Supervisor Sanction Pads. Trowbridge: Positive Press

Mosley, J (2012) Playground Rules. Outdoor durable wall poster. Trowbridge: Positive Press

Mosley, J (2012) Jenny Mosley's Playground Rules. Outdoor durable circles. Trowbridge: Positive Press

Mosley, J (2012) Learning through Action Posters. Trowbridge: Positive Press

Mosley, J. and Thorp, G. (2002) Positive Playtimes. Exciting ideas for a calmer school. Cambridge: LDA

Mosley, J and Thorp, G (2002) Playground Games. Cambridge: LDA

For information about the full range of Jenny Mosley's books and equipment contact:

www.circle-time.co.uk
email: positivepress@jennymosley.co.uk   Telephone: 01225 719204

Training Available from Jenny Mosley Consultancies

Jenny Mosley Consultancies provides courses to promote positive qualities and raise self-esteem. Most popular are our lunchtimes and playtimes courses. These courses support midday supervisors and everyone involved in lunchtimes and playtimes to transform this time of day into a haven of creativity and productivity.

Courses for Midday Supervisors

We believe that lunchtimes and playtimes are two of the most important times in a child's day and that our courses for midday supervisors:

- Are best for helping your whole school promote a positive lunchtimes policy;

- Encourage all the adults and children to organise and engage in creative play;

- Help everyone to get the most out of this time of day so that afternoons become calmer, more enjoyable and more productive.

Courses to Promote Children's Social and Emotional Skills

Research tells us that competencies such as empathy, motivation, understanding and managing feelings and getting along with others are crucial in explaining success in the classroom and beyond. We can bring training in the social and emotional aspects of learning into your school and transform the way it is delivered to:

- Help teachers make the most of their teaching opportunities;

- Make a real difference to the level of social and emotional skills;

- Promote positive behaviour and boost self-esteem.

For more information about training, contact: 01225 767157

Email: circletime@jennymosley.co.uk
Website: www.circle-time.co.uk

Follow us on Facebook, Twitter, Blog.